THE BRITISH MUSEUM Pocket Timeline of
Ancient Egypt

Helen Strudwick

THE BRITISH MUSEUM PRESS

© 2005 The Trustees of the British Museum

First published in Great Britain by British Museum Press
A division of the British Museum Company Ltd
38 Russell Square, London WC1B 3QQ

ISBN-13:   978-0-7141-3107-8
ISBN-10:   0-7141-3107-5

Helen Strudwick has asserted the right to be identified as the
author of this work.
A catalogue record for this title is available from the British
Library.

Designed and typeset by Peter Bailey at Proof Books
Printed in China

All photographs are © The Trustees of the British Museum,
taken by the British Museum Photography and Imaging Dept,
unless otherwise stated.

Map on page 31 by ML Design.
Werner Forman Archive: Unas pyramid photo in the Timeline.
Griffith Institute: p. 21 bottom.
© Graham Harrison/harripix.com: p. 7 top and bottom; p. 13
bottom; p. 22 bottom; Edfu temple photo in Timeline.
Helen and Nigel Strudwick: p. 8 top; p. 27 bottom; p. 30
bottom; photographs of Deir el Medina, Tanis and the mosque
in the Timeline.

CONTENTS

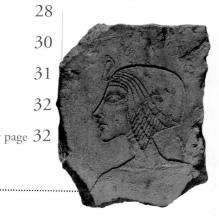

THE HISTORY OF EGYPT

THE ANCIENT EGYPTIANS recorded lists of their kings on papyrus and also on the walls of some temples. In the third century BC, an Egyptian priest called Manetho wrote one of the first histories of Egypt. He divided the kings up into dynasties (family groups). Modern historians still use the system of dynasties set down by Manetho and they group them into different periods or kingdoms. It can be hard to date events in ancient history exactly, and experts do not always agree. You may see slightly different dates in different books.

This book will take you through the history of ancient Egypt from Prehistory to early Roman times. You will see that many things stayed the same throughout that time, but many things changed.

Part of a king list from a temple of Ramesses II at Abydos. Some kings, who were thought to be bad rulers, were left out.

PREHISTORIC (PREDYNASTIC) EGYPT

7500 TO 3000 BC | FIVE THOUSAND years before the pyramids were built, Egypt's climate was much wetter than it is today. So the areas on either side of the Nile, which are now desert, were green with plants and trees and people could live there. These people used to hunt animals and gather wild plants for their food. People who live like this are called hunter-gatherers.

A prehistoric man from Gebelein whose body was naturally dried out by the desert sand.

FARMING AND SETTLEMENTS

As the climate became drier, people moved closer to the river Nile and became farmers. When they died they were buried straight in the hot sand, which dried out their bodies so that they did not rot away. We can understand a little about the way they lived from the objects buried with them. In about 3500 BC people began to make pots decorated with boats. From these, we can tell that the river Nile was already being used for travel.

EARLY HIEROGLYPHS

As people settled down together, they began to write things down, and the first hieroglyphic signs started to be used about 3400 BC. This period is also famous for beautiful objects made of stone, such as flint knives and stone jars.

A Predynastic pot.

An Egyptian flint knife.

ARCHAIC EGYPT, THE EARLY DYNASTIC PERIOD

This small ivory plaque shows king Den hitting an enemy with a mace. From this time onwards the kings of Egypt were regularly shown like this.

3000 TO 2686 BC AROUND 3000 BC, Egypt came under the control of one ruler. According to later legend the first king was called Menes, and he founded the capital city of Memphis. That name is not found on objects from this period, and it is likely that stories about Menes are based on two real kings, Narmer and Aha.

HORUS

The king's name was often written inside a rectangle, called a *serekh*, with a falcon on top. This was a symbol of the god Horus. The Egyptians believed that the king was Horus while he was alive. The kings of this period were buried at Abydos, which later became the sacred town of the god Osiris, the father of Horus.

At this time most buildings were made of mud brick and very few of them have survived. One of the most important towns of the period was at Hierakonpolis, where one of the first Egyptian temples was built.

A block of stone, called a *stela*, which marked the tomb of King Peribsen at Abydos. It is inscribed with a *serekh* containing his name. On top is a figure of the god Seth (the enemy of Horus). This may show that Seth and Horus were as important as each other at this time.

OLD KINGDOM

2686 TO C. 2160 BC The Old Kingdom was the great age of pyramid building. This began in the 3rd dynasty when king Djoser (2667–2648 BC) built a step pyramid at Saqqara, close to the capital at Memphis. It was the world's first monument made of stone.

The Step Pyramid of king Djoser at Saqqara.

PYRAMIDS AT GIZA

The largest pyramid, known as the Great Pyramid, is at Giza, and was built for king Khufu (also called Cheops, 2589–2566 BC). At this period the cult of the sun god Ra began to be important, and king Djedefra, who followed Khufu, was the first one to be given the title 'son of Ra'.

The pyramids of Giza.

Unlike Djoser's step pyramid, the pyramids at Giza were smooth on the outside. Most of the stone came from the area around the base of the pyramids, but the outer coating was usually made of high-quality limestone, which had to be brought from further away. King Menkaura's pyramid, also at Giza, was even planned to be coated with granite from the quarries at Aswan, about 985 km (600 miles) to the south.

A block of stone from the Great Pyramid.

Pyramids of kings of the 5th dynasty at Abusir.

Later pyramids in the Old Kingdom were not so large and they were also not built in the same way. Only the outside was made of stone blocks, while the interior was made of rubble.

PYRAMID TEXTS

The pyramid of king Unas (2375–2345 BC) had magical spells written on the inside. These are called the Pyramid Texts and many later pyramids were inscribed in the same way. The spells are intended to protect the dead king from danger in the afterlife. There were also prayers to be spoken during the burial ritual.

TOMBS AND MUMMIES

Government officials and other wealthy people were buried in tombs with chapels where offerings could be left for them.

This slab of stone comes from the tomb of Rahotep and shows him sitting in front of a table with loaves of bread on it. His figure is shown following the rules of ancient Egyptian art.

EGYPTIAN ART

By the time of the Old Kingdom the rules of ancient Egyptian art were set. These meant the artists did not try to create a natural-looking portrait of a person. For example, his or her head and lower body were shown as if seen from the side, while the shoulders were shown from the front.

Tomb chapels were often decorated with scenes showing day-to-day life and offerings being brought to the dead person.

During the Predynastic Period, the bodies of the dead were sometimes wrapped in linen and preserved with resin. During the Old Kingdom, this practice became more developed and it became normal for dead bodies to be carefully wrapped up, and even dressed with clothes, so that on the outside they seemed well preserved.

The Egyptians believed that their spirits lived on after death and that their preserved body would be the place where the spirits would regularly return. In case the body was destroyed, a statue was often placed in a special chamber in the tomb chapel.

A statue of a man and his wife from their tomb.

WRITING

Some very important early writings on papyrus were found in the buildings around the pyramid of a king of the 5th dynasty, Neferirkara. They are called the Abusir Papyri and give details about the offerings to be made to the dead king and the way the priests were organized. There are letters and permits, too.

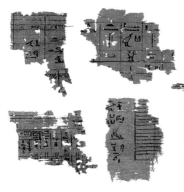

Part of a papyrus from Abusir.

SIMPLIFIED HIEROGLYPHS

Writing on papyrus with a pen led to the hieroglyphic signs being simplified. About 2700 BC a new form of writing appeared which Egyptologists call 'hieratic script' in which the signs have a much simpler form.

PEPY II

The last great king of the Old Kingdom was Pepy II. He reigned from about 2278 to about 2184 BC, more than 90 years. So he must have been very young when he became king. The rulers who followed after his death had only very short reigns and the organization of the country began to break up.

A statue of an official from around the end of the Old Kingdom. At this time officials who lived in the provinces started to become more powerful than they were before.

This slab of stone is called a false door. It was made for an official in the reign of Pepy II. It was put into his tomb to allow his spirit to pass between the worlds of the living and the dead.

FIRST INTERMEDIATE PERIOD

2160 - 2055 BC A FTER THE END of the Old Kingdom, there was no single king ruling the whole of Egypt. Instead, local governors set themselves up as rulers within their own regions.

Officials were still rich enough to afford to be buried in decorated tombs. These were often carved into the rock cliffs on either side of the Nile valley.

THE RISE OF THEBES

Gradually the local rulers of Thebes started to take control of large parts of southern Egypt. The First Intermediate Period ended when the Theban ruler, Mentuhotep II, came to the throne in 2055 BC. He became king of the whole country in about 2016 BC.

This stela belongs to a man called Inheretnakht. It may have marked the place where he was buried.

MIDDLE KINGDOM

2055 TO 1650 BC

Later Egyptians remembered Mentuhotep II as the king who brought the country back together after a time of chaos. He built temples in many parts of the country and he enlarged the temples at Karnak, which were dedicated to the god Amun and his family, and to Montu. On the opposite side of the Nile, he built himself a large funerary temple (a type of temple for looking after the spirits of the dead king in the afterlife). His wives were buried in the same place. Close to the temple is a tomb that contained the body of 60 soldiers who may have died during the fighting at the end of the First Intermediate Period.

Mentuhotep II, from Thebes in the south, is shown wearing the red crown of northern Egypt.

KINGS

The next important ruler was Amenemhat I, who was the first king of the 12th dynasty. He moved the capital city away from Thebes to a new city called Itjitawy close to Lisht, about 50 km (30 miles) south of Memphis near the Fayum.

He set up a new system of governing the different regions of Egypt using local mayors who were appointed by the king. His army pushed south into Nubia and also fought against the Libyans in the west. Two texts from this period suggest that Amenemhat may have been murdered.

The kings who followed continued the military expeditions against the Libyans and the Nubians. Senusret I (1956–1920 BC) built a fort at Buhen in Nubia to make this area secure. Other kings added more forts until a whole chain of them was built along the Nile south of Aswan. The Egyptians also began to trade with countries to the northeast of the Delta.

Amenemhat III ruled for about 45 years (1831–1786 BC). This was a time of peace in Egypt and the king built many monuments, including a huge funerary temple beside his pyramid.

The kings of the 12th dynasty were buried in pyramids that were built with a mud-brick core, rather than stone or rubble. The stone coating on the outside was removed for other building projects and since then they have been eroded by the weather.

A pendant in the form of a shell with the name of Senusret.

The pyramid of Amenemhat III at Hawara.

Painting from the tomb of a man called Djehutyotep.

MIDDLE KINGDOM TOMBS

Many of the tombs belonging to the officials of the Middle Kingdom were decorated with very lively paintings. The burials often included furniture, clothes and sandals and weapons, as well as magical objects such as figures of animals. There were also painted wooden models that show servants ploughing, baking bread, weaving linen, and so on. The Egyptians hoped that the models would come to life and work for them in the afterlife.

On the right hand side of this coffin is a map of the way into the underworld.

DECORATED COFFINS

In the Old Kingdom, coffins were rather plain, made of wood or stone. In the Middle Kingdom, however, they were decorated with pictures of objects for use in the afterlife. There were also texts on them, known as the Coffin Texts. These were adapted from the Pyramid Texts, with some special new spells. Another text called the Book of Two Ways was also painted on coffins. It was often illustrated with a map for guiding the dead into the underworld.

An ostracon (a flake of limestone used for writing) with part of the *Tale of Sinuhe*.

WRITING AND LANGUAGE

The language of this period, known as Middle Egyptian, became the standard 'classical' form of ancient Egyptian and it was used in inscriptions on monuments until the Roman period. Middle Kingdom stories, such as the *Tale of Sinuhe* and *The Shipwrecked Sailor*, were very popular even in later periods.

THE END OF THE MIDDLE KINGDOM

The last ruler of the 12th dynasty was a woman called Sobekneferu, who reigned for about four years. The kings of the 13th dynasty still used Itjitawy as their capital, but many of them reigned only for a short time. At the same time, settlers from Asia Minor were becoming a major power in the eastern Delta. The Middle Kingdom ended as Egypt began to split apart again.

This seal shows the name of queen Sobekneferu.

SECOND INTERMEDIATE PERIOD

Coffin of king Nubkheperre Inyotef of the 17th dynasty.

B Y ABOUT 1650 BC, the people from Asia Minor who had settled in the eastern Delta had become an independent group of people. They had their own kings and a new capital city at Tell el-Daba. They are usually called the Hyksos. It is possible that they introduced horses and the use of the chariot into Egypt.

BATTLES WITH THE HYKSOS

After a time, a dynasty of Egyptian kings from Thebes (known as the 17th dynasty) took control of the south of the country. A famous text, the Rhind Mathematical Papyrus, was written at this time and an inscription on the back refers to towns taken in battles against the Hyksos. King Seqenenra was probably killed in battle, but king Kamose and his brother Ahmose eventually defeated them.

Part of the Rhind Mathematical Papyrus. It was written about 1555 BC, but it says that it is actually a copy of a much older papyrus. The main text is something like a mathematical textbook for scribes.

NEW KINGDOM

1550 TO 1069 BC A FTER THE Hyksos had been driven out of Egypt, Ahmose became king of the whole country. The capital of Egypt was soon moved back to Memphis in the north.

The 18th dynasty kings originally came from Thebes, and that city remained important in the New Kingdom and afterwards. The temples at Karnak were enlarged and the priests who looked after the worship of the main god of the area, Amun-Ra, became prominent people. Many new temples were built and they show that Egypt was a very wealthy country at that time.

A shabti figure belonging to king Ahmose.

Amenhotep I was the king who ruled after Ahmose. He was very popular in Thebes.

A statue of Amun-Ra from an unknown temple.

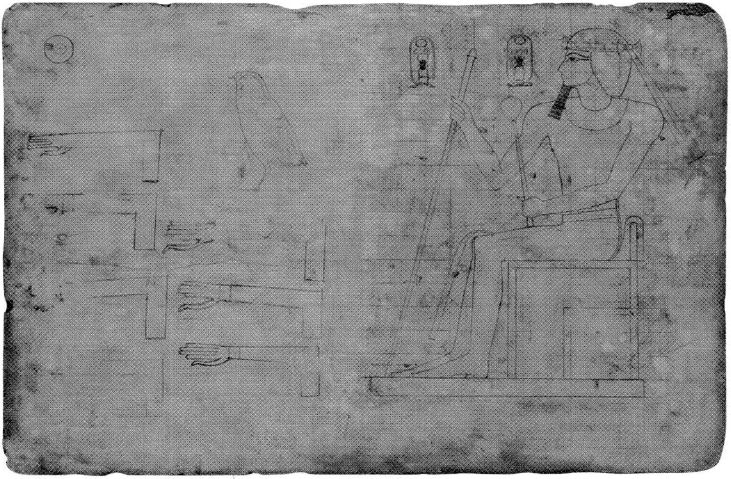

A wooden board used by an artist for practising drawing. The figure on the left is Thutmose III.

EGYPTIAN EXPANSION

The kings sent out their armies to conquer neighbouring countries and Egypt controlled large parts of Asia Minor and Nubia. Many foreign goods were brought into the country including large quantities of gold from the Nubian mines.

At the same period another country called Mitanni, which was in the area of modern Syria, was becoming stronger. After a time war broke out between the two countries. King Thutmose III (1479–1425) defeated them at the battle of Megiddo in 1456 BC.

HATSHEPSUT

Thutmose was quite a young man when his father died and so for the first few years he was supported by his step-mother, Hatshepsut. In the 7th year of his reign, Hatshepsut decided to become a king (not a queen) in her own right. She died in about the 22nd year of Thutmose's reign and was buried in a tomb in the Valley of the Kings. She also built a funerary temple next to the old one of Mentuhotep II, who was still remembered as a famous king at that period.

Architectural splendour

Amenhotep III (1390–1352 BC) was the greatest builder of all the Egyptian kings. His buildings are found in almost every part of Egypt and especially at Thebes, which must have been one huge building site during his reign. His architect was a man called Amenhotep son of Hapu, and in later times he was treated as a holy man. He even had his own funerary temple on the west bank of the Nile.

Cliff tombs

Kings were no longer buried in pyramids. Instead, they chose a hidden valley in the cliffs at Thebes as their burial place. Today this is known as the Valley of the Kings, and it contains the tombs of many of the kings of the New Kingdom. The walls of most of the tombs are covered with paintings and texts about each king's journey with the sun-god through the underworld.

A special team of workmen were employed to create the tombs. They lived in their own small town called Deir el-Medina quite close to the Valley of the Kings. As well as their houses, the government provided them with food and servants. In their spare time they built their own tombs and probably also tombs for officials in Thebes.

A statue of the goddess Sekhmet, which was made for the funerary temple of Amenhotep III at Thebes.

Some of the most beautiful objects and wall paintings were produced at this time. Most of these come from tombs, but they allow us to see how people lived, the clothes they wore and the furniture from their houses.

A stool made of black wood (ebony), with ivory decoration. The seat was leather which is less well preserved.

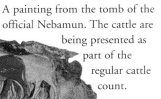

A painting from the tomb of the official Nebamun. The cattle are being presented as part of the regular cattle count.

SHABTI

During the Middle Kingdom, small statues called shabtis began to be included in burials. By the early New Kingdom they were equipped with tools for working in the fields. A magic spell was inscribed on them so that they would come to life if their owner was asked to work in the fields. This spell was part of the Book of the Dead, which was often written on a papyrus scroll and included in burials to help the dead to get safely into the afterlife.

A shabti figure from the early 18th dynasty.

The Amarna look

The art of the Amarna Period is easy to recognize because the human figures all have elongated heads and thin necks. Their bodies are also shown as rather paunchy but with long, thin arms and legs.

The Aten

The king who followed Amenhotep III was called Amenhotep IV (1352–1336 BC). In the 5th year of his reign he changed his name to Akhenaten. At the same time he promoted a new god, called the Aten, and closed the temples of the old gods. The capital was moved to a new town called Akhetaten, at the modern site of Amarna. Egyptologists call this the Amarna Period. His wife, Nefertiti, appeared on monuments with her husband.

A piece of stone with the image of a king from the Amarna period.

The old gods return

In about 1336 BC Tutankhaten became king. During his reign, he changed his name to Tutankhamun and reopened the old temples. When he died (1327 BC), he was buried in a small tomb in the Valley of the Kings which remained almost undisturbed until it was discovered in 1922 by Howard Carter and Lord Carnarvon.

Tutankhamun's mummy as it was found in its coffin.

The kings who followed tried to destroy the monuments of the Amarna period. Many objects from the time are damaged, with the royal names and pictures cut out. The last king of the 18th dynasty was Horemheb, who had been Tutankhamun's general.

THE RAMESSIDE PERIOD

The first king of the 19th dynasty was called Ramesses. He had been a general in the reign of Horemheb. Many of the kings who followed were called Ramesses and so this part of the New Kingdom is called the Ramesside Period.

His most famous successor was Ramesses II (1279–1213 BC), whose name is found on monuments throughout Egypt. Many of these monuments had been built by earlier kings and Ramesses II simply replaced their names with his own. However, he also set up many new building projects, including a new capital city at a place called Piramesse in the eastern Delta.

THE HITTITES AND THE 'SEA PEOPLE'

By this time, the Hittites had become the most powerful people in Asia Minor. Ramesses II went to war against them and on many of his monuments he was shown as being victorious at the battle of Qadesh. Hittite documents record the battle as a victory for their side, too, so it seems that neither side really won. Later, the two sides made peace and Ramesses II married a Hittite princess.

Ramesses II reigned for 66 years. He was succeeded by his 13th son, Merenptah (1213–1203 BC). During his reign Egypt came under attack from the 'Sea Peoples'. These people came from the north and passed through Asia Minor looking for places to settle. They joined forces with the Libyans and invaded Egypt.

A statue of Ramesses II holding a table for offerings.

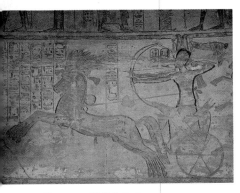

Ramesses II fighting at the Battle of Qadesh.

Merenptah was able to drive them back, but they attacked Egypt again during the reign of Ramesses III (1184–1153 BC). The king sent his army against them and his victory was recorded in his funerary temple at Medinet Habu in Thebes. Records show that one of his wives led a plot to murder him, but his mummy shows no sign of violence and it is not clear how he died.

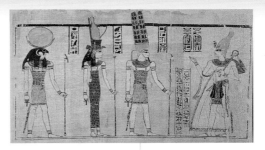

Ramesses III with the gods of Thebes. This is part of a huge papyrus that records events from the king's reign.

THE END OF THE NEW KINGDOM

The last king of this period, Ramesses XI, ruled from the north of Egypt. At the same time, the High Priests of Amun at Thebes became very powerful until they began to rule the south of Egypt. Once again Egypt was no longer controlled by a single ruler and the New Kingdom came to an end.

The face of the coffin of Ramesses VI. The rest of the coffin is still inside his tomb in the Valley of the Kings.

Part of a papyrus of the Book of the Dead showing the dead in the Field of Reeds. This scene was included in tomb paintings during the Ramesside period.

THIRD INTERMEDIATE PERIOD

1069 TO 716 BC

The kings of the 21st dynasty (1069–945 BC) ruled in the north eastern Delta from a new capital called Tanis. They were also buried in that city inside the enclosure walls of the main temple. Their tombs were found by archaeologists in 1939 and many had not been robbed.

THE PRIESTS OF AMUN

In the south, the country was ruled by the High Priests of Amun who were also generals. They ordered the bodies of the New Kingdom kings to be taken from their tombs and buried in two secret places. This may have been to protect them from being damaged by tomb robbers, or it may have been to strip the tombs of the wealth stored inside them.

During the Ramesside period, many Libyan families settled in the Delta. From about 984 BC many of the northern kings had Libyan names and probably came from these settlers. This part of Egyptian history is often called the Libyan period.

The god of the river Nile was called Hapy. This statue was inscribed by king Sheshonq II.

One of the great kings of the Third Intermediate Period was Sheshonq I (945–924 BC). He took control of Thebes by making one of his sons the High Priest of Amun. He also invaded southern Palestine. This is recorded in the Bible where his name is Shishak. His victories are recorded in inscriptions at the temple of Amun-Ra at Karnak.

DEMOTIC SCRIPT

At this time a new form of writing was developed. This is known as 'demotic script'. The signs it uses are even simpler than the hieratic ones and it would have been much quicker to write.

After Sheshonq's reign, the kings in the north became weaker and the organization of the country began to break up again. By about 730 BC there were several kings ruling at the same time: two in the Delta and two in the south.

THE RISE OF NUBIA

From about 750 BC, the rulers of Nubia gradually took control of southern Egypt, even reaching as far north as Thebes. About 730 BC one of the northern kings, Tefnakht, sent his troops south against the Nubian king Piye. They were defeated and Piye marched north as far as Memphis. After the northern kings accepted that Piye now controlled Egypt, he marched back south to Nubia. It was Piye's brother, Shabaqo, who finally brought Egypt back under the rule of one king in 716 BC.

Coffin of a man called Pasenhor. During this period, many more people could afford to be mummified after death. Usually these burials did not have a decorated tomb chapel. Instead the coffins were often beautifully decorated.

Canopic jars which would have contained the organs removed from a body when it was mummified.

LATE PERIOD

716 TO 332 BC I N 716 BC KING Shabaqo of Nubia conquered Egypt. He showed his loyalty to the Egyptian gods by renewing their temples and making new statues. Memphis was the capital of Egypt again, but the kings were buried in small pyramids in Nubia hundreds of miles further south.

The god Amun in the form of a ram protecting king Taharqo.

At this period the Assyrians were becoming powerful in the Near East. King Taharqo (690–664 BC) fought them several times as they tried to conquer Egypt. The Egyptians were finally defeated in 663 BC by the Assyrians, led by king Ashurbanipal.

EGYPT REGAINS CONTROL

The first king of the 26th dynasty was Psamtek I (664–610 BC) whose family came from Sais, a town in the Delta. He hired Greek soldiers and they helped to take Egypt back from the Assyrians. He also built a series of forts to protect the border in the northeast.

A new town for Greek settlers was built at Naukratis in the Delta in about 630 BC. Visitors from Greece became the first tourists to Egypt.

The kings of the 26th dynasty built many new temples in Egypt. They encouraged the worship of animals that were sacred to particular gods.

WAR WITH PERSIA

In 525 BC the Persians invaded and conquered Egypt and formed the 27th dynasty. They were led by Cambyses who showed respect for Egyptian religion. For example, he took care to see that the sacred Apis bull was correctly buried during his reign.

A king worshipping a bull called the Apis, which was sacred to the god Ptah. It was treated with great honour while it was alive and mummified and buried in a special tomb after it had died.

There were often rebellions against the rule of the Persians and they lost control of Egypt in 404 BC. During the next dynasties, powerful Egyptian families fought each other and struggled to rule the country.

The last great king of the Late Period was Nectanebo I (380–362 BC). He was able to defeat the Persians who tried to take control of Egypt again. After this there was a period of peace. Nectanebo renewed many of the main temples and added inscriptions and decoration to them.

At Karnak, Nectanebo II started to build a huge new gateway at the entrance to the temple. He died before it was finished.

The Persians invaded Egypt again in 343 BC. Egyptian records say that the Persians broke into the temples to steal their wealth and that they killed the sacred Apis bull, but this might not be true. We do know that the Egyptians hated them and they were happy when Alexander the Great conquered them and came to Egypt.

PTOLEMAIC PERIOD

Marble head of
Alexander the Great.

332 TO 30 BC IN 332 BC ALEXANDER the Great drove the Persians from Egypt and became ruler. A year later, he founded a new Mediterranean port – Alexandria.

THE PTOLEMAIC PERIOD

After Alexander's death in 323 BC his empire broke up, and Egypt was controlled by a general called Ptolemy. He declared himself king Ptolemy I in 305 BC. He was followed by 14 kings with the same name. This is called the Ptolemaic period.

Greek started to be the official language, but Egyptian was also used so that the local people could still understand documents.

ANIMAL CULTS

The Ptolemies expanded many of the old Egyptian temples, and built some new ones. They continued the customs of the old religion, including the many animal cults.

Mummified falcon. The person who paid for the fine bandaging and bronze mask was showing great devotion to the falcon god Horus.

During the reign of Ptolemy IV, the southern part of Egypt tried to become independent. His son, Ptolemy V, was only 6 years old when his father died and he became king in 204 BC. He was very generous to the temples and in 196 BC the Egyptian priests wrote a decree honouring him. The decree was inscribed on the Rosetta Stone three times: in two forms of Egyptian (hieroglyphs and demotic) and also in Greek. When the stone was found, about 2,000 years later, it became one of the keys to deciphering the ancient Egyptian language.

ROMAN ASCENDANCY
Gradually the Ptolemies became weak kings. The Romans were becoming the strongest power in the region and they started to try to take control of Egypt.

The last queen of Egypt was the famous Cleopatra VII (51–30 BC). Her brother, Ptolemy XIII, tried to become king instead of her, but Cleopatra was helped by the Roman leader, Julius Caesar, who made her queen again, ruling together with her half-brother Ptolemy XIV. She later married Mark Antony who wanted to be the next ruler of Rome. They both committed suicide after the Battle of Actium when Mark Antony was defeated and Egypt became a province of Rome.

The Rosetta Stone.

Cleopatra's face on a coin of the time.

ROMAN PERIOD AND LATER

A statue of the god Thoth in the form of a baboon from the Roman period.

FROM 30 BC

IN 30 BC THE emperor Augustus became the first Roman ruler of Egypt. None of the emperors ever lived there and Egypt was no longer the independent country it had been. It was forced to send grain to Rome as a tax.

TRADITIONAL CUSTOMS

The Roman emperors added many buildings to the old temples and there were carvings showing them as traditional Egyptian kings. The last hieroglyphic inscription was written in AD 394.

The Egyptian custom of mummifying the dead continued. In the Fayum, the mummies were given portraits of the dead person painted on wood, which were bound in with the linen wrappings.

RELIGIOUS CHANGES

Egypt became a Christian country during the 4th century. Then in AD 641–2 the Arabs conquered Egypt and brought the religion of Islam to Egypt. Today Egypt is a mainly Muslim country, although there are still many Christians, called Copts, in parts of the country.

A portrait from a Roman mummy.

A small building at the temple of Isis at Philae, built by the Roman emperor Trajan (AD 98-117).

■ AD 180
Alexandria becomes a centre of the Christian religion in Egypt.

■ c. AD 280
St Antony founds the first monastery in the world.

■ AD 303
The emperor Diocletian tries to destroy Christianity.

■ AD 306-337
Constantine I becomes emperor and the Roman empire, including Egypt, becomes Christian. Egyptian Christians are called Copts.

The gravestone of a Coptic person called 'Young Mary'.

■ AD 394
The last inscription in hieroglyphic script is inscribed on a wall at the temple of Isis at Philae.

An early Islamic mosque built inside an ancient Egyptian temple.

■ AD 641-2
The Arabs come to Egypt bringing their religion, Islam, with them.

300 BC TO AD 1

The Rosetta Stone, inscribed with a decree of the priests for Ptolemy V in 196 BC.

A small building at the temple of Isis on the island of Philae near Aswan. It was built by the emperor Trajan (AD 98–117).

■ **205 BC**
The area around Thebes tries to become an independent state.

■ **204–180 BC**
Reign of Ptolemy V. He regains control of the south of Egypt and is very generous to the temples.

■ **c. 170 BC**
The Romans begin to interfere in the government of Egypt.

■ **51 BC**
Cleopatra VII becomes queen of Egypt.

Coin of Cleopatra VII.

■ **48 BC**
Cleopatra VII's brother, Ptolemy XIII, tries to remove her from power, but the Roman leader, Julius Caesar, helps Cleopatra to become queen again.

■ **41 BC**
Mark Antony comes to Egypt and forms an alliance with Cleopatra.

■ **31 BC**
Mark Antony is defeated at the Battle of Actium by Octavian, who later changes his name to Augustus.

■ **30 BC** Mark Antony and Cleopatra commit suicide and the Roman emperor, Augustus, takes control of Egypt.

The Roman emperors do not live in Egypt and it is no longer an independent country.

Many buildings are added to the old Egyptian temples.

The Egyptian language starts to be written using Greek letters, with a few demotic signs. This new form of writing is called Coptic.

The Romans were interested in the Egyptian religion. This figure is the Egyptian god Horus dressed in Roman armour.

600 BC TO 300 BC

■ 525–404 BC
The Persians control Egypt.

■ 380–362 BC
Reign of Nectanebo I, who renews many of the old temples and adds new buildings to them.

■ 343–332 BC
The Persians conquer Egypt again. The Egyptians say that they are treated very harshly.

At Karnak, king Nectanebo I started to build a huge new gateway at the entrance to the temple. It was not quite finished when he died.

A king worshipping the sacred Apis bull.

■ 332 BC
Alexander the Great comes to Egypt and becomes its new ruler.

■ 331 BC
A new city is founded at Alexandria.

■ 323 BC
Alexander dies and Egypt comes under the control of his general Ptolemy.

■ 305 BC
Ptolemy declares himself king of Egypt.

Greek becomes the official language of government, but hieroglyphs and demotic are also used.

The Ptolemies expanded the old temples and built new ones, such as this one at Edfu.

A mummified falcon.

750 BC
The Nubians enter the area of Aswan and start to move northwards.

730 BC
King Piye of Nubia defeats the northern king of Egypt, Tefnakht. He then returns to Nubia.

Scribes begin to use a new form of writing called 'demotic'. The signs are much simpler than those used in hieratic and much quicker to write.

716 BC
The Nubian king, Shabaqo, comes to Egypt and becomes king of the whole country.

Memphis becomes the capital of Egypt again.

674 BC
The Assyrians invade Egypt. They are defeated by king Taharqo.

A statue of the god Amun, in the form of a ram, protecting a small figure of king Taharqo. This statue comes from a temple that the king built in Nubia.

Demotic writing on a papyrus.

671 BC
The Assyrians attack again and capture the city of Memphis.

663 BC
The Assyrians capture Thebes and control the whole country.

664–610 BC
Reign of Psamtek I, who takes Egypt back into the control of the Egyptians.

Cults of sacred animals are very popular.

1200 BC TO 900 BC

■ 1184–1153 BC Reign of Ramesses III. The Sea Peoples and the Libyans attack Egypt and Ramesses defeats them.

■ 1099 BC Ramesses XI takes the throne. He is the last king of the New Kingdom.

■ 1080 BC General Piankhy becomes High Priest of Amun and rules the southern half of Egypt.

■ 1069–715 BC Kings of the 21st and 22nd dynasty rule in the Delta. Some of them are Libyans.

The south of Egypt is controlled by the High Priests of Amun.

The coffin of a Libyan man called Pasenhor.

The face of the coffin of Ramesses VI. Other parts are still inside his tomb in the Valley of the Kings.

Tanis, capital city of the Delta.

The tombs of the kings are inside the temple at Tanis.

■ 925 BC Sheshonq I tries to take control of Palestine.

Coffins are very beautifully decorated with religious scenes.

1500 BC TO 1200 BC

NEW KINGDOM 1550 – 1069 BC

18th-20th Dynasties

■ 1500 BC
Valley of the Kings becomes the new burial place for the kings of Egypt.

A team of craftsmen is assembled for building the kings' tombs. A special town is built for them to live in.

■ 1456 BC
Thutmose III leads his army into Asia Minor to confront the people of Mitanni. He wins a victory at Megiddo.

Tombs are cut into the cliffs and hills on the west bank at Thebes for officials. They are decorated with beautiful carvings and paintings.

The village of Deir el Medina, home of the workers from the Valley of the Kings.

■ 1352–1336 BC
Reign of Amenhotep IV/Akhenaten. He closes the old temples and makes the Aten the most important god in Egypt.

■ c. 1336 BC
Tutankhamun becomes king and restores the cults of the old gods.

An Amarna king.

■ 1279–1213 BC
Ramesses II builds a new capital city in the Delta at Piramesse. He wages war against the Hittites, especially at the Battle of Qadesh.

■ 1213–1203 BC
Merenptah defends Egypt against the Sea Peoples.

A statue of Ramesses II holding a table for offerings.

A painting from the tomb of Nebamun.

1800 BC TO 1500 BC

■ **1773–1650 BC**
The kings of the 13th dynasty gradually lose control of the country.

■ **1650–1550 BC**
Foreigners, often called the Hyksos, start to rule the eastern Delta where they have settled. They build their own capital city at Tell el-Daba.

Horses and chariots may have come to Egypt at this time.

■ **1580–1550 BC**
17th dynasty kings from Thebes build up their forces and try to drive the Hyksos out of Egypt.

Many hippopotamus figures were made at this time.

A scarab from the burial of a king of the 17th dynasty.

■ **1550 BC**
Ahmose becomes king in Thebes. He defeats the Hyksos and takes control of the whole of Egypt.

A shabti figure belonging to king Ahmose.

The capital of Egypt moves back to Memphis.

The Theban god Amun becomes one of the most important gods in Egypt.

Figurine of Amun.

2100 BC TO 1800 BC

MIDDLE KINGDOM
2055 – 1650 BC
11th-14th Dynasties

■ c. 2016 BC
King Mentuhotep II of Thebes defeats other rulers and becomes the king of the whole of Egypt.

Thebes becomes an important city. Mentuhotep enlarges the temples at Karnak.

■ 1985 BC
Amenemhat I becomes king. He moves the capital city north to a new city close to Lisht.

Local mayors are appointed by the king to rule the provinces.

Mentuhotep II wearing the red crown of northern Egypt.

Egypt begins to expand southwards into Nubia.

■ 1956 BC
Amenemhat I dies, possibly murdered. He is succeeded by Senusret I.

Painting from the tomb of a man called Djehutyhotep.

Local governors decorate their tombs with paintings showing how rich and important they are.

Models of servants at work were included in tomb equipment.

The kings build forts in Nubia to control this area.

■ 1831–1786 BC
Egyptian art reaches a high point during the reign of Amenemhat III.

Classic stories like *The Shipwrecked Sailor* and *The Tale of Sinuhe* are written.

Kings of the 12th dynasty are buried in mud-brick pyramids.

2400 BC TO 2100 BC

A coffin made of granite, which was found in a tomb at Giza.

■ 2375–2345 BC
King Unas. Rooms inside his pyramid are inscribed with magical spells, now called the Pyramid Texts.

Pyramid texts on the inner walls of the pyramid of Unas.

■ 2160–2055 BC
Egypt is divided, with several kings ruling from different parts of the country.

■ 2125–2016 BC
Rulers at Thebes from the 11th dynasty become strong and start to control large parts of Egypt.

A false door from the tomb of an official in the reign of king Pepy II.

■ 2278–c. 2184 BC
Pepy II reigns for more than 90 years.

Governors in the provinces become more powerful than they had been before.

■ 2184–2160 BC
Many kings reign for only a short time. The organization of the country breaks up.

An inscription mentions the temple of the god Amun at Karnak for the first time.

A stela (gravestone) of a man called Inheretnakht.

■ **2667–2648 BC**
King Djoser builds the first pyramid at Saqqara. This is the first use of stone for a large building project.

■ **about 2700 BC**
A simplified form of writing, based on hieroglyphic signs, starts to be used for writing on papyrus. It is known as hieratic script.

A piece of plaster from the wall of a tomb with a painting showing a man feeding an antelope.

The pyramids at Giza.

■ **2589–2566 BC**
Life of Khufu, who builds the Great Pyramid at Giza. It is the biggest pyramid ever made and is built of stone.

The sun god Ra becomes important during this period.

Government officials are buried in tombs with decorated chapels.

■ **2494–2184 BC**
Pyramids are built of rubble, with a coating of stone on the outside. This makes them cheaper to build.

3000 BC TO 2700 BC

ARCHAIC PERIOD 3000 BC – 2686 BC
1st-2nd Dynasties

■ 3000 BC
Egypt is ruled for the first time by one king, later known as Menes.

■ 3000–2686 BC Early kings are buried in mud-brick tombs at Abydos.

Ivory plaque showing king Den smiting an enemy.

Kings are associated with the god Horus.

THE BRITISH MUSEUM
Pocket Timeline of
Ancient Egypt

THIS TIMELINE TELLS you all the main events from the history of ancient Egypt and about the people who lived there. The timeline is divided into sections of 300 years, apart from the first and last sections. The first one deals with ancient Egypt before 3000 BC, and the last one covers the period from AD 1 to AD 642.

Egyptian history is usually divided into periods, such as the Old Kingdom, the First Intermediate Period, and so on. These periods are shown in the coloured strip at the top of the timeline, just below the dates, and you can find out more about them in the book.

BEFORE 3000 BC
PREHISTORIC AND PREDYNASTIC 7500 – 3000 BC

■ 7500 BC
Early Egyptians live in the desert areas, which are green at this time.

■ c. 5450-4400
Farmers start to grow forms of wheat and barley and to keep animals nearer the Nile.

■ 4400–3200 BC
People begin to bury their dead in pits in the sand.

■ c. 3400 BC
First use of hieroglyphs.

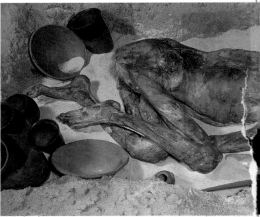

A Predynastic pot.

A prehistoric man whose body was dried out by the desert sand.

FURTHER READING

THE BRITISH MUSEUM ILLUSTRATED
ENCYCLOPAEDIA OF ANCIENT EGYPT
Geraldine Harris and Delia
Pemberton
British Museum Press, 1999

GODS AND PHARAOHS FROM
EGYPTIAN MYTHOLOGY
Geraldine Harris
Bedrick, 1993

LIFE IN ANCIENT EGYPT
Eugen Strouhal
Cambridge University Press, 1992

For older readers:
THE CULTURAL ATLAS OF
ANCIENT EGYPT
John Baines and Jaromir Malek
Facts on File, revised edition 2000

DEATH AND THE AFTERLIFE IN
ANCIENT EGYPT
John H. Taylor
British Museum Press, 2000

The following **websites** are also
good places to find information
about ancient Egypt:

**www.thebritishmuseum.ac.uk/
compass**

www.ancientegypt.co.uk

**www.bbc.co.uk/history/ancient/
egyptians/**

www.newton.cam.ac.uk/egypt

MAP

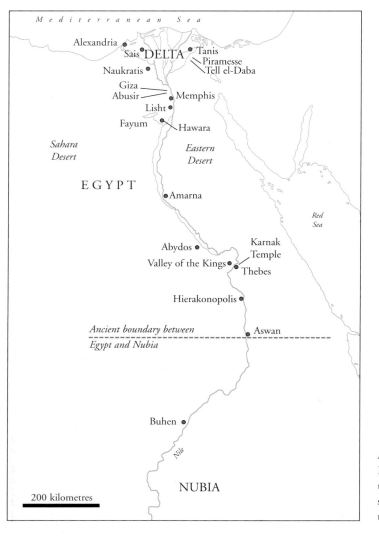

A map of ancient Egypt, showing the important sites mentioned in this book.